YOUR KNOWLEDGE HAS VALUE

- We will publish your bachelor's and master's thesis, essays and papers

- Your own eBook and book - sold worldwide in all relevant shops

- Earn money with each sale

Upload your text at www.GRIN.com
and publish for free

Carol Nganga

An Application of JIT and Lean Operations in a Manufacturing Company

GRIN Verlag

Bibliografische Information der Deutschen Nationalbibliothek:

Die Deutsche Bibliothek verzeichnet diese Publikation in der Deutschen National-bibliografie; detaillierte bibliografische Daten sind im Internet über http://dnb.d-nb.de/ abrufbar.

Dieses Werk sowie alle darin enthaltenen einzelnen Beiträge und Abbildungen sind urheberrechtlich geschützt. Jede Verwertung, die nicht ausdrücklich vom Urheberrechtsschutz zugelassen ist, bedarf der vorherigen Zustimmung des Verlages. Das gilt insbesondere für Vervielfältigungen, Bearbeitungen, Übersetzungen, Mikroverfilmungen, Auswertungen durch Datenbanken und für die Einspeicherung und Verarbeitung in elektronische Systeme. Alle Rechte, auch die des auszugsweisen Nachdrucks, der fotomechanischen Wiedergabe (einschließlich Mikrokopie) sowie der Auswertung durch Datenbanken oder ähnliche Einrichtungen, vorbehalten.

Imprint:

Copyright © 2012 GRIN Verlag GmbH
Druck und Bindung: Books on Demand GmbH, Norderstedt Germany
ISBN: 978-3-656-73948-7

This book at GRIN:

http://www.grin.com/en/e-book/280539/an-application-of-jit-and-lean-operations-in-a-manufacturing-company

An Application of JIT and Lean Operations in a Manufacturing Company

Globalization of businesses has provoked the development of international supply chains. A Supply chain manages all the activities aimed at meeting the customer needs and maximizing the effectiveness of the process. This process starts from the extraction of raw materials to the customer receiving the finished good. Its aim is to satisfy the customer. Supply chain management aims at the company achieving a sustainable competitive advantage. This has initiated the application of just-in-time systems.

Just-in-time is an inventory scheduling technique. It was developed as an operations control and planning philosophy that assisted manufacturers attain consistent improvement in quality of products and productivity of the processes. JIT encompasses stock less production and zero inventories. It broadly focuses on elimination of waste from producing more than is required, waiting time, waste on transportation cost, inventory, processing and product defects throughout the organization.

JIT philosophy encompasses the following principles. The first principle is the operation excellence which requires the organization to be committed to continuous process and product improvement at all departments focusing on proper customer services. The second principle is value added processes which ensures that those processes that add no value to the customer or product are eliminated as they only add on cost of production; every aspect of the processes in the organization should be aiming at continuous improvement. Lastly, JIT techniques are focused towards total quality management and empowerment of employees (Ross, 2004).

JIT techniques

Being the manager of a company that involves itself in the manufacture and marketing of personal computers, I am to incorporate the use of JIT and lean operations in the company. The income statement, balance sheet and balance scorecard will form the basis of my simulation. The pro forma statements and the budgets are conservative but very strategic. The company's biggest worries were cash flow and debt level. It disregarded future productions and investments. Some of its operations were closed to save on money as the competition was not that high. The company did not take count of the probability of competition being experienced in the future.

Just in time focuses on efficient throughput, reduction in inventory and waste. The computer company took this a little bit far too far where it closed some of its operations. Closure of certain operations reduces the sales volume to the end of the last quarter. The competition was negligible but the computer company did not put into consideration global market strategies and future investments seriously. Waste was eliminated by maximum utilization of operating capacity. Leaving the plant that was closed could also have the company's JIT increasing its throughput that took to move orders receipt to their delivery in other countries (Cheng & Poldosky, 1993).

Implementation of Just in Time technique would be by having suppliers who were supportive. If the company reduces the number of suppliers, it will facilitate the delivery of raw materials on a timely basis. This would also ensure the supplies are delivered to the specific work places. A work cell-based layout and machinery that were flexible would be an appropriate move. Proper organization of workplaces and reduced inventory spaces would ensure effective and efficient operations by the company.

Inventory being managed in small sizes, specialized part bins, and allocation of low setup time would be implemented. The operations should not deviate from the planned schedule. Each operation should be allocated a level schedule and suppliers notified of the existing schedule in the firm. A schedule on preventive maintenance with the operator being involved daily would also be implemented. Being a manager, I would also implement quality production based on statistical control of the process, suppliers who offer nothing less than quality and quality production in the firm too.

Another strategy I would implement is the empowerment of employees, training of support staff and employees. This would increase efficiency in production. Classification of fewer jobs would also ensure that employees are more flexible. I would also be committed to supporting the company's management, its employees and suppliers.

Application of JIT aims at significant cost savings by the company. Employee training will improve on the quality of finished goods and a reduction in waste levels. The reduction in cost of production would also impact on the prices of our products. Prices which are lower would be set, increasing the sales level. These techniques would also reduce the cost by lowering the occurrences of rework. Variable production cost would also be on the decline. These factors above would be of great significance to the customer through reduced cost and delivery of high-quality products.

Lean operations

Lean operations involve the elimination of activities that do not add any value to the production activities and also to customers from the supply chain. Lean operations philosophy applies the same strategies used by JIT. Lean operations philosophy has incorporated elements such as elimination of waste which is essential in JIT. Waste does not add value o the production activities and therefore it is important to eliminate it. Just like JIT, it aims at creating a new culture which encourages all employees to involve themselves in the continuous improvement of production activities and generate new ideas that improves and performs a number of functions in the organization. Lean operations also adopt the continuous improvement element of JIT. This philosophy believes it is likely to attain the ideals of JIT through continued improvements over time.

A well-managed operation management leads to lean production. Lean production focuses on the customer while as JIT is focused on the internal operations. An understanding of what the customer preferences and wants are important to lean production. The manager should also have a platform where the customers give their feedback about the products they purchase from the company. Therefore, lean operations are all about identification of customers value by conducting an analysis of all activities involved in the production process. Optimization of the production process from what the customer perceives the product is the final stage.

An organization that focuses on JIT, empowerment of employees and quality of products are a good example of lean producers. Through these, organizations can drive out those activities that have no value to the eyes of the customer. Lean operations are helpful in minimizing waste as it focuses on the production of the best products to customers through continued learning, teamwork and creativity in firms.

To ensure operation efficiency in the manufacturing company, I would apply JIT techniques. Application of JIT assists in the elimination of inventory. Elimination of virtually all inventories is possible where the company produces according to customer's demands thus creating free space. These free space in the company, which can be used to perform other activities instead of stocking all warehouses with inventories. Manufacturers can train employees to work in different departments or workstations thus reducing on idle labor. Having a well trained flexible workforce reduces cost of operations and improves on satisfaction of the customers needs.

Employees in the company are to be educated on the importance of understanding the needs of the customer. An understanding of customer needs will ensure that employees produce a perfect part every time an order is placed. This will reduce the cost of production through rejected goods as a result of low quality products. To achieve these, employee empowerment, commitment of employees and teamwork will be emphasized.

Lean operations will also be incorporated in the manufacturing company by developing a close relationship with the suppliers. This creates a favorable environment for conducting business. Being the manager of the company, I will ensure that suppliers understand the customer's needs and obligate them towards the achievement of customer needs. This will make the suppliers feel to be part of the supply chain.

Operation efficiency

The application of JIT and lean operations will help the company achieve operational efficiency through a reduction in waste. Waste in the company is as a result of overproduction, delays in delivery of raw materials to company and final products to customers, defects in products and employees who are poorly trained. Application of JIT in our company will lower the cost of production and increase productivity by half the initial production. A reduction in inventory will improve on the operational efficiency of the company as the idle space will be used for other activities in the production process. This will be possible by proper training of the employees to be able to work in different production points. An improvement in quality of production and elimination of non value-added costs increases operational efficiency of the company. This will attract more customers to the firm as quality products and customer satisfaction is key thus a well-built competitive advantage.

References

Cheng, T. C. E., & Podolsky, S. (1993). *Just-in-time manufacturing: An introduction*. London: Chapman & Hall.

Ross, D. F. (2004). *Distribution: Planning and control : managing in the era of supply chain management*. Boston: Kluwer Academic Publishers.